ZEN BODHISATTVA

THE PRAJNA-PARAMITA WAY

VOLUME FOUR

ZEN BODHISATTVA

THE PRAJNA-PARAMITA WAY

VOLUME FOUR

MICHAEL DEAN PAYNE

authorHOUSE®

AuthorHouse™ UK
1663 Liberty Drive
Bloomington, IN 47403 USA
www.authorhouse.co.uk
Phone: 0800.197.4150

Published by AuthorHouse 09/23/2015

ISBN: 978-1-5049-9144-5 (sc)
ISBN: 978-1-5049-9143-8 (e)

Print information available on the last page.

This book is printed on acid-free paper.

Dedicated to the life of all beings...

The way...

Preface

The original Zen master, Bodhidharma, walked into
China, with one of his sandals on his head.
A large crowd had gathered, including the emperor, to greet him.
Bodhidharma, ignored the whole crowd and walked
past but was stopped by the emperor, who pleaded with
Bodhidharma."Please tell me, what merit have I attained, through
my own effort, to build countless temples in my land?"
Bodhidharma, spoke directly, saying, "no merit at all!"
Shocked by Bodhidharma's words, the emperor
asked, "who are you to say such a thing?"
Bodhidharma, spoke directly again, saying, "I know not!"
Bodhidharma, continued walking alone, found a cave to live
in, alone, and faced the wall in silence for around nine years.
Eventually, Bodhidharma, accepted to share the way of Zen,
with a few who had shown true potential, to realise the way.
One man, took out a large blade, and with one stroke,
cut off the flesh and muscle from his own forearm.
This was to show Bodhidharma, his pure
intention to become a disciple of Zen...

Introduction

Enlightenment is a destructive process,
it is the crumbling away of untruth,
it is the letting-go of everything you held to be true...

~

Through the raging fire of wisdom,
the flaming blade of awareness is forged.
Through mastery of the sharpness, of its blade,
the empire of the desire realm is hacked to pieces.
This is realised through stillness, within silence.
The continuous practise of zazen, silent sitting meditation,
and the continuous practise of koan, an open question,
given through master to disciple,
to penetrate the depths of the mind,
to be free of all conditioned realities,
to realise the extinguished state of perfect enlightenment...

The Silent Temple

The master of Zen, sparkles with enlightenment.
His silence teaches disciples, both inside and outside the temple.
The whole temple itself stands in silence,
without any noise at all...

Koan practise

Koan, is an open question, given through Zen master,
to disciple. The function of koan, is for the disciple to
breakthrough the appearance of obstacles in the mind, to
destroy delusion and suffering, enabling the disciple to realise
the capacity to see the path of perfect enlightenment.
The disciple may work with a single koan throughout his or her
entire life, offering an answer to the master at each meeting.
If the answer to the koan remains imperfect then the disciple is
sent away after every meeting to continue working with the koan.
Koan, allows the master and disciple to be in a pure relationship
together. The master looks through the disciples mind directly,
and is fierce in the way the disciple is trained to perfection of
realisation, of the way, of Zen. See **Blissful Anvil – Story of
a Bodhisattva who remained still – volume three...**

Zazen practise

Zazen, is silent sitting meditation. Observing breathing and
sensation, without reacting to appearances of the mind or body.
The aim of the practise is to realise silence and stillness,
without being distracted by inner or outer phenomena,
of form, sound, smell, taste, touch, or thought.
Zazen, involves your whole action, of body, speech, and mind,
together. Through sitting, walking, cleaning, eating, working,
and so on, your whole life becomes the meditation practise...

~

Still and moving,
Zen is pure silence...

One koan,
is enough to transform the mind into a blacksmith's anvil.
Enough to break all hammers...

Why does the man inside the hermitage,
not know what is going on outside...

When a true koan is dropped in truth,
your whole identity breaks into pieces.
All that remains is the wind that cannot be seen...

Why is my hand like a Buddha's hand,
why is my foot like a donkey's foot...

How does the temple floor sweep it's self...

Where is dust in the first place...

The only obstruction appearing in the mind,
is identity...

If you understand words,
can you understand silence...

Silence is not the absence of sound,
silence is the absence of self...

More Zen in a quiet dog,
than any theory...

Do not make a sound,
unless it adds to silence...

What is there to say that has not already been said...

Above all,
may silence make you strong...

Where is your true-self,
Show it to me...

What have you tried to be in the past,
what are you trying to be in the future.
What have you let go of now...

How do these senses exist,
of form, sound, smell, taste, touch, and thought...

Who is reacting to what...

What is the sound of water...

What is the difference between knowing the path,
and walking the path...

Where is your true being...

Emptiness

Emptiness, is the clear middle way.
Zazen, is living the direct middle path.
Thoughts, feelings, and emotions, are formless.
Actions are performed through awareness of this present moment.
Not in the past, not in the future.
The meditation of the middle way, is Zen, in everything
you do. Sitting, walking, cleaning, eating, working.
Your doing, is your meditation.
See the flow without owning the space...

If you avoid silence,
can noise avoid you...

Ten Perfections, Of The Bodhisattva Way, Of Enlightenment

Perfection Of Giving
Perfection Of Moral Disciple
Perfection Of Patience
Perfection Of Effort
Perfection Of Concentration
Perfection Of Wisdom Of Ultimate Truth
Perfection Of Skilful Means
Perfection Of Prayerfulness
Perfection Of Force
Perfection Of Wisdom Of Conventional Truth

~

Practising all ten perfections, together, within the same moment.
The Bodhisattva realises, from giving to perfection.
There is, no-self, giving, no-gift, no-self receiving.
In this way, The Bodhisattva, realises all ten grounds
of perfection, seeing clearly and directly.
Without relying upon any subject or object, of
form, sound, smell, taste, touch, or thought.
Without any sense, of-self, person, living being, or life span.
The True Bodhisattva, walks the path of perfect enlightenment.
Taking the suffering of all beings,
whilst giving the victory of realisation...

Perfection Of Giving
Realise giving, in a pure way, with a pure mind

Perfection Of Moral Discipline
Realise pure action, of body, speech, and mind, together

Perfection Of Patience
Realise this moment

Perfection Of Effort
Realise effortlessness

Perfection Of Concentration
Realise stillness

Perfection Of Wisdom Of Ultimate Truth
Realise silence

Perfection Of Skilful Means
Realise seeing, clearly and directly

Perfection Of Prayerfulness
Realise selflessness

Perfection Of Force
Realise fearlessness

Perfection Of Exalted Wisdom Of Conventional Truth
Realise formlessness of appearances

The Bodhisattva Vow

Beings are limitless, **I vow to save all beings.**
The suffering of beings is endless, **I vow**
to destroy all suffering.
The Great Dharma is immeasurable, **I**
vow to realise all Dharma.
The Buddha path is unsurpassed, **I vow to realise**
the perfect path of enlightenment.

~

Just as all the previous Buddhas,
generated the mind of enlightenment,
and accomplished all the stages of the Bodhisattva training,
so will I too,
for the sake of all beings,
generate the mind of enlightenment,
and accomplish all the stages of the Bodhisattva training...

~

The Pratimoksha Vow

To refrain from killing
To refrain from stealing
To refrain from sexual misconduct
To refrain from lying
To refrain from using intoxicants

~

The Pratimoksha Vow, is a promise to abandon contaminated
actions, of body, speech, and mind. This Vow is a practise of
training in moral discipline, to realise liberation of the causes of
suffering, and establish the foundation to practise in truth...

THE PRAJNA-PARAMITA WAY

The Great Dharma, is the heart of the Bodhisattva, The Buddha is within this. Everything is, The Great Dharma. True Bodhisattvas, do not get caught in appearances, nor does a Bodhisattva hold onto any notions, of perception, of concepts, of ideas, of ideals, of images, or of idols.

Subjects and objects still appear in a conventional way but Bodhisattvas do not get caught in ordinary appearances, or in the emptiness of ordinary appearances.

A true Bodhisattva, sees everything as, The Great Dharma. All subjects and objects are within this, Great Jewel. It is rare to realise such a treasure as this, it is truly beyond measure.

A Bodhisattva, does not hold any self-belief, or perceive any belief in a person, a living being, or a life span. A True Bodhisattva, does not abide in any notion of life or death, but disappears into cherishing all who appear to suffer, with the pure intention to destroy the appearance of suffering for the true benefit of all without exception.

The essence of a Bodhisattva is great compassion and profound wisdom, whose only intention is to destroy suffering for all who appear to suffer. Bodhisattvas train within the ten perfections, not for themselves alone but for everybody who appears to experience suffering without exception.

True Bodhisattvas train within all ten perfections together, within the same moment, every moment, without wasting a moment.

The spirit of a Bodhisattva is like a vast fertile ground, the soil of their mind is free of weeds, thorn bushes, and stones.

There are no obstructions in the clear mind of a Bodhisattva, such as, selfishness, anger, attachment, or ignorance, so, only the seeds of perfect enlightenment grow within the fertile soil of a Bodhisattva's mind.

The Buddha sees this clearly and directly, this is why the Buddha always shows support and confidence in the Bodhisattvas.

The flow of the Buddha's presence, through the Dharmakaya body, is enough to water the seeds of perfect enlightenment to grow within everybody whom the Bodhisattva is with. This shows the inexhaustible energy and pure awareness of both the Buddha and Bodhisattva together because there is no perception of separation or difference because both realise the same pure intention.

"Bodhi," means awakened or enlightened. "Sattva," means essence. Bodhisattvas connect with everybody on the path of awakening without exception because everybody has the seed of perfect enlightenment.

The Bodhisattva's whole intention is to touch everybody's mind in a subtle way to allow the seeds of perfect enlightenment to grow, sowing the seeds of the Bodhisattva mind within everybody to allow everybody to realise perfect enlightenment and become a living Buddha.

This is the pure function of **The Prajnaparamita Sutra.**

"Prajna," means ultimate truth or ultimate awareness. "Paramita," means perfection. "Sutra," means teaching. (This small part of the original Sutra), offers clear guidance on how a Bodhisattva should master their thinking through practising the ten perfections of the Bodhisattva way of perfect enlightenment...

~

THE PRAJNAPARAMITA SUTRA

The Buddha said to Subhuti, "This is how the Bodhisattva Mahasattvas master their thinking. However many species of living beings there are, whether born from eggs, from the womb, from moisture, or spontaneously, whether they have form or do not have form, whether they have perceptions or do not have perceptions, or whether it cannot be said of them that they have perceptions or that they do not have perceptions, we must lead all these beings to ultimate nirvana so that they can be liberated. And when this innumerable, immeasurable, infinite number of beings has become liberated, we do not, in truth, think that a single being has been liberated."

"Why is this so? If Subhuti, a Bodhisattva holds onto the idea that a self, a person, a living being, or a life span exists, that person is not an authentic Bodhisattva."

~

Bodhisattva Mahasattvas, are fortunate enough, to receive, accept, practise, and realise, The Bodhisattva Vow. "Maha," means Great. The Great Vow, is taken with great compassion and profound wisdom, to destroy the suffering of all beings, and to offer all beings the victory of absolute nirvana, perfect enlightenment.

A True Bodhisattva does not realise this for their self, Bodhisattvas do not perceive a self in any form. The whole foundation of the Bodhisattva way, is to care for all beings in a loving way and to destroy all appearances of suffering.

This Great Vow, is seen to be of the greatest importance and responsibility, seeing this Great Vow, as a wishfulfilling jewel that fulfills the wishes of all beings without exception.

The Great Vow, is taken as a devoted promise to take the suffering of all beings and offer ultimate peace and joyfulness.

A Bodhisattva gives rise to a mind that is not based upon anything. True Bodhisattvas, have vowed to dedicate their whole lives to the service of all others who appear to suffer without exception.

All Great Bodhisattvas give rise to purity of mind in this way, giving rise to a mind that is not based upon any form, a mind that is not based upon any sound, a mind that is not based upon any smell, a mind that is not based upon any taste, a mind that is not based upon any touch, a mind that is not based upon any thought.

Pure consciousness has no foundation, the perfect enlightenment of a Buddha, contains everything and so it has no base...

Awareness does the profound work, not you.
Through silence and stillness,
you can listen and see the way.
None of this, is held, known, or owned, by you.
Everything and everybody, is a blessing.
When giving to perfection, realise,
you are not the giver, you are not the gift, you are not the receiver.
When helping others, who appear to suffer,
do not stand in the way.
Allow awareness to do the work through you, to show the way.
Speak directly, in a clear way.
Remain selfless, with clear heart and clear mind.
Without clouds, of thoughts, feelings, or emotions.
Do not react to the mundane activity of your own mind,
do not fool yourself through your own ideas of belief.
Be fierce in your daily practise, without desire for a self.
Be pure in your action,
always generate great compassion, and wisdom together.
Through this awareness, all things appear clear and direct...

How do you realise where you are...

Is everything transparent in truth...

Carrying the 84,000 teachings, is useless.
Lapping-up the fox slobber of preachers, is worse.
How many crooked fingers do you need to point to the moon,
when everything disappears into emptiness...

If you lap-up the fox slobber of preachers,
can you sit and chew your own food in silence...

Water is a great teacher...

True questions and answers,
appear when serving all beings together...

Are we all in this together...

Practise what you see...

Respect the truth...

Is there anything to offer to help you,
is there anything to take away...

What do you see,
why do you see it...

How do you see the path...

Is your reality clear...

Do you walk alone or with a crowd,
what is the clear direction...

Through quiet contemplation and serene reflection of these works,
may the direct path be used in the clear way,
for the true benefit of all beings together without exception...

Michael Dean Payne

September 2015

For more details please contact:

peacewarrior74@hotmail.co.uk

The essence of, **ZEN BODHISATTVA,** offers the true disciple the clear way to train through the direct path of zazen meditation and koan practise, through realising all ten perfections of, The Bodhisattva Way Of Enlightenment through **The Prajnaparamita Sutra.**

All four volumes are a practical guide, offering the clear contemporary way to walk the ancient direct path of perfect enlightenment. Each volume offers a glimpse of my life experience of suffering, and insight of awareness, through my daily meditation practise. Through the great compassion and profound wisdom of, The Bodhisattva Way, the true disciple realises the way of taking the suffering of all beings and giving the victory of realisation, to enable all beings the capacity to see how to be free of the causes of suffering...

Michael Dean Payne, lives in Lytham St Annes, England. He has trained in, The Bodhisattva Way Of Enlightenment, for many years. He has dedicated his life to helping everybody who appears to suffer in the world and offers everybody the way to release themselves and others of their own suffering, together, through realisation. This is seen clearly and directly, throughout all four volumes, written and published to enable everybody the capacity to see the direct path to journey through life that will clearly benefit everybody together...

~

EXPLOSIVE AWARENESS VOLUME ONE

Introduction to awareness of compassion and wisdom

~

BLISSFUL LANTERN VOLUME TWO

Introduction to the daily practise of Silent Awareness Meditation

~

BLISSFUL ANVIL VOLUME THREE

Introduction to The Bodhisattva Way Of Life

~

ZEN BODHISATTVA VOLUME FOUR

Introduction to The Bodhisattva Way Of Enlightenment

Lightning Source UK Ltd.
Milton Keynes UK
UKOW04f0118210116

266794UK00002B/190/P